I AM A DIAMOND

A JOURNAL AND PLAYBOOK FOR LIFE

PAMELA A. MAJOR

I AM A DIAMOND

A JOURNAL AND PLAYBOOK FOR LIFE

PAMELA A. MAJOR

I AM A DIAMOND
@2018 by Pamela Major

NewSeason Books and Media
PO Box 1403
Havertown, PA 19083
www.newseasonbooks.com
newseasonbooks@gmail.com

TABLE OF CONTENTS

DEDICATION

I truly dedicate this playbook to each and every reader. You are ALL valuable and you ALL have sparkle and shine. Find it, live it, and give it!

I want to give a special dedication to Leila, Mekhai, Talia, Oni, Clever, Niyah, Zion, Ayla and Reign...my princess cousins. Each of you are diamonds; precious, unique, and shielded with love. Each of you has made my heart expand so I am able to love more.

To Adra,
Be unashamed to
sparkle & shine!

06.29.18

INTRODUCTION

Being an introvert, I enjoy talking with myself. I ask questions, develop thoughts, and ultimately, make decisions. As the result of my intentional personal growth over the years, I have developed an excellent and healthy internal dialogue. I have more balance when I consider situations, issues and people. But in truth, this took (and takes) work. It is not automatic. I essentially created and took a "course" in discovering me. I wasn't trying to be special, unique or deep, I was just trying to be me. The God kind of me. The one He always intended.

I was already good at talking to myself, but soon the question became "what am I saying and does it really help?" If I wanted to be more comfortable with myself from the inside out, then I had to come to the realization that my words and thoughts didn't always help and that God's always would. *That* journey started about five years ago, and I was delighted to find out what God had to say about me. Learning and rehearsing God's word over my life has, well, expanded my living. It has allowed me to take that internal dialogue and live a transformed life. I invite you to do the same. Use this "life playbook" on your own journey of discovery. Find out and embrace what God says about you. Don't rush through it. Sit and drink in the word. As you develop your "plays," I'm absolutely certain you will look at the bible with renewed adoration. You will thank God for revealing all the good and wonderful things He has to say about you.

Matthew 22:37-40 teaches us to love God and love people as (or in the same way) as we love ourselves. How do you love *you*? How do you treat you? What do you say to yourself about yourself? These are questions you will answer on this journey. Knowing how well you love yourself will offer you a picture of how well you love others.

We often confuse self-love with selfishness and vanity. Nothing could be further from the truth. Self-love ignites forgiveness, mercy, and grace for you, and then for others (loving our neighbors as ourselves). It sparks all of those wonderful attributes found in 1 Corinthians 13: patience, kindness, not being boastful, NOT keeping a record of wrongs and NEVER giving up. True self-love results in looking into the "mirror" of self and finding the balance between giving yourself a break and recognizing when you have done the wrong thing. True self-love finds the strength to apologize and operate differently—even if that apology is to you.

I want you to know that I don't have all the answers. What I can do and what I desire to do is to share pieces of my life--my trials and triumphs—in hopes that they will guide you toward your own personal victory.

I often use the term *virtual mentor* to refer to people who I admire and learn from, but do not have a close relationship with. I heard one of my virtual mentors, Dr. Cindy Trimm, use this phrase once: "I took care of the issues in my tissues a long time ago." What I believe she was saying is that she came to know herself, deal with her past, shed her pain and embrace what God had to say about her above and beyond anything else. The next question for many of us is usually, "How?" That was my question. I wanted to know *how* to get to that point. Maybe you do too. Well, another virtual mentor of mine, Bishop T.D. Jakes, answered our "how" questions like this: "I can understand you not studying calculus, but I don't understand you not studying you."
That's the starting point. That's where I began and where I think you should start also. Getting to know me was one of the most important things I would ever do.

I recently was describing to a friend an exchange I had with someone that bothered me greatly. After I finished my rant, she asked me a question that initially challenged me, but as I continued "studying" myself, made sense. She said, "When you know yourself, you know (and admit to) your triggers." Knowing yourself can (and will) stop you from "pulling the trigger" and unloading, misinterpreting, and mishandling others.

It gave me peace to understand myself and it stopped me from doing harm to others by verbally alienating or assassinating them. The journey to getting to know myself and what God says about me, stopped me from being toxic in my judgements. I learned to *wait out* more situations. I also became sweeter. Getting to know the Christ in you, should make you sweeter.

We all start out somewhere when we meet Christ. We all have a story, a challenge. Our personal challenges reveal themselves in different ways though. Not everyone has a drug, sex, or shopping addiction. Not everyone is a thief, pimp, or hustler. Some of us are so "mild" in our presentation that most people won't see our issues. But we do have them and we do need God to help us just as much. I looked like a capable, yielded, and willing worker for the Lord. That was right on the surface. But underneath was a woman looking for approval and thinking that using my gifts, talents, and abilities would get me the validation my heart desired.

Like I said, we all come with something.

No matter what you came to Christ with, there are at least three things that are true: 1) we all have our thing, 2) God is willing to work with us, and 3) we all can be transformed. All we need is some one on one "coaching" with God, the Father. No one knows you better or is more willing to share who you are with you. This, I know for sure. My hope is that you will dive in and do this unafraid. But even if you are afraid—do it anyway!

This journal is intended to be both journal and playbook. Decide to jump into this as an adventure. It is made to be picked up and put down. As you make the "plays," practice them. There are many questions, scriptures, thoughts and declarations I've included on this journey. It is my hope and prayer that these words and guided questions conclude in you definitively declaring I AM A DIAMOND—and walking in the fullness of that revelation.

1

PLAYBOOKS AND DIAMONDS

I have the unique pleasure of growing up as a parent's girl. I know that sounds strange but I never had a stronger leaning toward one parent or the other. I had wonderful, equally strong connections to both my mother and father. I am a solo child (spoiled, but not rotten) and given to cherishing the wonderful uniqueness that comes with leaning with equal weight on my adoration for both mom and dad. It was and is special.

With my mother, I revel in the memories of tea parties, perfume splashing, and nail painting weekends. Some of my other joys were playing dress up and walking while balancing a book on my head (great posture was a requirement in my home). These bonding moments with my mother were priceless. I loved looking through fashion magazines with her, selecting colors, and watching her create design magic (all with no formal education—it was one of her God given anointings).

The bond with my father was equally powerful even if the activity list was much different. My father loved history, politics, and debate. He loved conversation, creating theories and solutions, and particular to this journal, he loved football. I mean he *loved* football.

Dad played in high school, briefly in college, followed by the military and then just for fun until he could physically no longer. Most significantly, he was a football coach. He coached for the recreation department in our city for about 20 years. Back then, it was called midget football (I know it is politically incorrect now, but that was the name then) which was similar to Pop Warner. Through bonding with my father, I learned about playing the game of football and I learned plenty about...you guessed it...playbooks.

If you are thinking, "well, that's not my experience," hold on, here's the great news! Maybe your experience growing up did not include this type of bonding. Maybe your relationships with your father and mother were strained or non-existent. It's OK. It really is. Because no matter what, God never leaves us without His love. The bible says, "Even if my father and mother abandon me, the LORD will hold me close" (Psalm 27:10 NLT). So take heart! The LORD is still holding you close and will still reveal to you some plays for living. On the other side of this, you will be revealed and unleashed as the powerful, polished diamond he designed.

Playbook for Life?

A playbook is a series of constructed and strategic moves based on assignments designed to either score points or defend territory. While there are several assignments, each of them is represented by one symbol for offense and a different one for defense. The usual symbols that represent assignments in a football playbook are "Xs" and "Os." As a woman of faith who is absolutely into symbolism, this screams Jesus to me. Let me explain.

In a football play, an X represents a defensive player. The player that is charged with defending territory. The is one who says "you will not gain one inch of ground here. I will protect this territory to the death." This is where it gets exciting (even if you don't like or understand football). In the Greek language (the language of the New Testament) the X stands for the letter Chi (pronounced Ky); this letter represents Christ (This is why we see X-mas. It's not a shortcut or an elimination of Christ, but similar to you or I calling a dear friend by their first initial). And who is the ultimate defensive player?

Exactly.

Christ has defended us to the death and back to life. He is absolutely on our team. As a matter of fact, Jesus is the team captain. When the enemy of our souls attempts to attack us, our Defender is there fighting on our behalf.

Offense is where the player seeks to gain territory. It's where we score points. The language of "scoring" might make some feel uncomfortable but think of it as the things we do as believers to advance the Kingdom. On the offensive side, an "O" or circle represents the player in a playbook. The circle is a symbol of covenant. Because of the covenant we have with God, we can advance the kingdom. With him, we always win.

The challenge of the playbook?

US.

Will we make the plays God has given us? Will we seek him to know what to do and how to do it? Will we yield ourselves, our will, in favor of his? He often has a way of doing things that are different from the way we live. This is why we must renew our minds (see Romans 12:1-2). It is a matter of choice.

Let's go deeper.

I want to point out that whether our lives are on offense or defense, we are covered. God shows us that Christ covers us and his covenant stands forever. That said, we must invest in knowing what God, the Father, has to say about us. One of our greatest strategies for accomplishing this is taking the time to come away and hear. When we set aside our past, put away our routines, and choose "God-fidence" (the strength and power that comes when we place the full weight of our faith in God's love and promises), we are more powerful than we can imagine. In our weakness, we are made strong (see 2 Corinthians 12:10).

I hope that as we explore these analogies of creating plays for your life and recognizing your value as God's precious jewel, you remember that whether your territory is being defended or you are advancing into purpose and vision, Christ is with you. One of the most important things you can do to advance your play is to understand just who you are:

You are a diamond. You are being exposed, cut, shaped, and set. You are a reflection of the love of God wherever you go. So with this book as your guide, and through prayer and meditation with the Father, begin to develop some plays that keep you in remembrance of this.

There are three things I would like you to consider doing as you go through the process of making your plays. Each must be a part of every play you make whether you are advancing or defending. You must make a decision, a decree, and a declaration.

A Decision, a Decree, or a Declaration

I wrote this journal because helping others has been planted in my heart from before I was born (see Jeremiah 1:5). As a five year old, I knew I wanted to do something with my life that would help others and that remains a part of my purpose. In my conversations with God, and as I arise from my moments of challenge, question or grief, I always believe that my journey may help someone else who is enduring the same or similar trials. You are holding in your hands (or reading from your electronic device) a decision that became a decree that has allowed me to share this declaration to you: I am (and you are) a Diamond.

This book is a decision, a decree and a declaration.

A decision:

"And God said let there be light and there was light" (Genesis 1:3).

"In the beginning was the Word and the Word was with God and the Word was God. He was in the beginning with God...The Word became flesh and made his dwelling among us" (John 1:1-2, 14a).

God has modeled for us a pattern of turning the abstract into the concrete; turning thoughts (intangible things) into realities (something you can see, feel, taste, etc.). There are so many examples of this in scripture and yet we often miss it. I don't want you to miss it any longer so let's connect the dots! Consider all of these verses that speak to the connection between our thoughts (abstract) and our reality (concrete):

"We were as grasshoppers in our own eyes, and we looked the same to them" (Numbers 13:33 NIV)

"The tongue has the power of life and death; and those who love it will eat its fruit"(Proverbs 18:21a NIV)

"This is what the Sovereign LORD says to these bones: I will make breath enter you and you will come to life" (Ezekiel 37:5 NIV).

"For as a man thinketh, in his heart so is he" (Proverbs 23:7a KJV).

Each of these verses demands we make a decision. How do we see ourselves (as lowly grasshoppers or being able to overcome adversaries and live in the land of promise)? Will we eat the fruit (results) of life or of death with the words we speak? Will we receive or reject the life giving breath of God? How do we think in our hearts, in our inner most being (self/soul)? What are our secret internal and guiding thoughts? In other words, what are our established "plays" and what kind of victory are we getting from them? Too often we are guided away from using the power of the Word and the power given to us by using our own words and aligning them with God's.

Many of us have lived under what I consider a dangerous myth. Our well meaning parents/loved ones shared a little saying in hopes of keeping us from harm. They'd already experienced the ways people can hurt others and wanted to help us. They taught us to say, "sticks and stones may break my bones but words will never harm me." As I said, they meant well, but this was an incredible misguidance.

If words can create the world and everything in it (go back to Genesis), and since they can become flesh (see John 1), why wouldn't they be able to harm us? The truth is…words can absolutely harm you. Look at the passages of scripture above. If life and death are in the power of the tongue, we have to understand that the negative, life sapping, defeating words we speak—not to mention the words we *accept*—can do us great harm! The reverse is also true. The good words we *accept* and the evil words we *reject* can offer us great health and wholeness. It is our choice whether we want to make the latter our new play.

These new plays come from both God's word and the time you spend with him. These are the plays you will use to build your God-fidence. These plays can become your meditation, your self talk, and what fills you to the overflow. Knowing, acknowledging and accepting how precious you are to God gives you a courage and humility that is unstoppable. I want you to be unstoppable.

As you read the subjects in this journal, and see how closely your life mirrors the qualities and characteristics of a diamond, you have to make a choice either for you or against you. A choice to believe what God has said about you or to turn away from it. I invite you to invest in the decision making process. I invite you to read and embrace what God, the Father says about you and ultimately, I invite you to make the decision to choose what he says over anything else you hear. Notice life and death are in the same place—your tongue. You get to decide.

To decide is to settle an argument; a dispute. To decide is to cut off all other options and settle on one. I pray you decide to settle on your God given authority to make a choice for life and blessings instead or death and cursing (see Deuteronomy 30:19). When you make the decision, move on to the next step. The next step is to make a decree.

A decree:

"You shall also decree a thing and it shall be established for you; And light will shine on your ways" (Job 22:28 NASB).

A decree is a legal term. It references the decision of a governing body (in this case YOU). Out of all the options, all of the possibilities, and all of the evidence presented to you, a decision was made. Now is your time to formalize this decision and turn it into a law for your life; a decree. You may ask, "How can I do that?" Well, the answer is, you are already doing it. You are acting out in your life the sum total of the unwritten, unspoken, and unconscious laws of your life. All the things you experience and accept, get filtered through what you believe and become your personal set of living laws. They inform every response you make, in every situation. What I am inviting you to do is to make conscious choices about those laws. You have a God given authority to make the changes you need for your life.

I am inviting you to use God's word as the defining factor of every law in your life. Take a deep dive into the love letter that is God's word, the bible, and examine the patience God has with you but also the love he has for you. Soak in all the not so subtle clues he provides about living a good life.

The decree is an invitation to define your change. When we change, we must be clear about it, comfortable or otherwise. Sometimes (well, quite often) there is a time of wrestling with the change. More than I'd like to admit, I will try to find a way to change without changing. I will go through the stages of grief over the thing that I must release from my life. I try to act like change isn't needed (denial). I get angry, I bargain somewhere, I even get depressed. In the end, I accept the change and go about stating the way I am going to live, act, and be. It is certainly a process, but ultimately, I get excited. I think of my new way of living and consider the great things it will bring; the heaviness I am leaving behind.

Truthfully, not everything feels like heaviness. Yes, there are people and ideas we'd like to hold onto. This journey is not about being a perfect person, it's about being a yielded one! So we get our tissues and cry our cries, then we remember: God knows what's best for me. We get together in the "huddle" and create the decree.

This journal and playbook has prompts, information and questions that will allow you, the reader, to invest in some one-on-one self-assessment. In some of the chapters, you'll find a *His Word/My Thoughts* section. Here is where it will be **up to you** to go into the bible and see what God says. Search for scriptures that align with what you've just written. Write those scriptures down, memorize them, and meditate (personalize and internalize it). Repeat it to the point where it replaces the old "law" governing your life. Also, do some activities to reinforce the new law. Write it down or post it in the notes function of your phone. You might consider putting it on your mirror or refrigerator. It may seem silly, but heavy rotation is a great strategy. It works! Think about all the song lyrics you know. That's a perfect example of heavy rotation. Making the decree means you not only memorize the words, but you become intimate with them to the point where there are results. Having a law, a decree, also means you are familiar with the consequences of breaking the law. You know what happens when you return to old habits, ways, and limiting beliefs. As yourself if that's what you really want.

Now let's move on to the part that can both excite and expose you. Our next step, the declaration, is part of this process.

A declaration

When a decree is created, it is shared publicly in a declaration. Like the Declaration of Independence or a President's executive order, a declaration shares publicly what we hope has been considered and constructed privately. It is the decision made and the decree agreed upon now gone public.

A declaration brings clarity and light. A declaration shares all the things you figured out in private. When I am going through, it's easy to lose clarity. Things become very dark. When I do not focus, or I focus on the wrong thing, I end up saying the wrong things. I create a world where I speak what I do not want, imagine what I fear most, and embrace the worst case scenario. However, making a declaration reminds me of who I am, who made me and the truth of what he (God) says about me. My declaration brings light. God's word brings light (see Psalm 119:130). When I agree with Heaven, situations change, starting in my mind and continuing in my thoughts.

When you make the decision and decree to yourself who you are, you must make a declaration. Declarations show up in your speech and your response to outside forces. Your declaration is not complete until the change becomes your new normal. What will you do differently? How will you shift? How will you make your comeback when you slip? Who can you trust with your difference? Who will hold you accountable?

God wants us to team up with people. Community serves many purposes (see Ecclesiastes 4:9-12). We have the opportunity to partner with colleagues, friends, teammates, siblings, and spouses. And sure, there are times when even those closest to us don't get us. I had a situation where I shared my hurt with a dear friend. This friend heard my story much differently than I shared it. My pain became their pain. It was terrible. This is where discernment is key. We should serve and share our stories in community. But there will be times when it's more appropriate to share your deepest fears and personal concerns with God and God alone. Rest assured, he will never misinterpret you.

I look at God as the ultimate partner. He is always on target. He knows where he wants you to go and how to help you get there. He is always doing his part in our lives, so it is up to us to do ours. So I ask you, will you dare to team up with the ultimate partner? One way to initiate this partnership with him is through the process of journaling.

The point of journaling

Journaling has become a critical tool for me. Sometimes writing things out helps me to realize the truth, develop a resolution, and rid myself of pains, afflictions, and self-limiting or defeating habits. It is a place to house the tears shed along the way and the lessons each salty drop provides.

Journaling is totally about you! It is about what is on your mind. It tracks where you have been, where you are, and where you want to go. It is a personal place to share your thoughts and travels. It can be a place of reasoning and reality. Your journal is a blank slate waiting for you to fill it with your dreams and visions. It takes what is in your heart and mind and provides a place and space to download. There is something unique about the physical use of your hand as it connects with your mind, the untouchable location of your thoughts and the activator of your brain. Your journal becomes the place where you develop and fine tune the "plays" of your life.

As you go through the pages and exercises in this playbook and journal, you will find a great deal of space. This is by design. As I mentioned, there is something about writing things down in your own hand and connecting your thoughts in a tangible format. It is like taking the abstract and making it concrete. Writing your thoughts helps to make them material and leaves a record. Your thoughts here about yourself, your journey, your significance, all factor into your success; a success that is both broad and narrow. It's broad in the sense that we all have some measure of success, but narrow in that what you are assigned to do is specific to you. You are fearfully and wonderfully made and there is no other like you. Your mold was broken and there is only one you!

As you move through each of the chapters and begin writing your thoughts, consider the following:

- Always know what you are trying to advance or defend.
- Tap into how you have handled this kind of matter in the past and the results
- Think about the godly principle that you need to apply
- Write what you think
- Decide, decree, declare.

One more thing

You are striving for intentional growth. You will use what you have, to go on to achieve more, learn more, even lead more. It's not about being an overachiever, it is similar to what Paul says in Philippians 3. You are "pressing toward the mark for the prize of the high calling of Jesus Christ " and the journey lasts a lifetime.

This is an opportunity for cleansing and refreshment that will help you experience growth and transformation. Each of us has layers of protection—culture, traditions, expectations—hiding our authentic selves. These layers unwittingly and unwillingly become a cocoon, of sorts. Now it is time for you to choose a new cocoon filled with God's word creating a perfect environment for the "butterfly" you to emerge.

***

What do you think?

Here is a great opportunity to write your first thoughts, expectations and hopes as you enter this journey

_____

_____

_____

_____

_____

_____

_____

_____

_____

_____

_____

_____

_____

Prayer

Father, you have given your Word to help me. Let me go into it with new eyes. Allow me to see things about me that you want me to know. Let me see your instruction, your ways and most of all your love for me. I am open to your voice and desire to know more about how you see me.

2

FROM PRESSURE TO PRECIOUS: THE PROCESS

Process.

It's actually a legal term that means moving forward and advancing. When a case is processed, a person is put on trial and evidence, laws, even witnesses are brought forward. This is a metaphor for our own growth. The process we endure in our lives is the opportunity to learn the life lessons (evidence) that come about in the time between where you are (laws) and where you're going (the desired case outcome). It's the prize of the journey. It can't be avoided or ignored. Without going through a process, we become stagnant and unable to achieve victory. The process that God allows us to experience in our lives, propels us into becoming the full expression of ourselves. It is worth the unknown events, separations, and pain that can come along with it.

Writing this playbook has been part of my process. I always wanted to be a writer. I was already a talker, debater, and asker of questions. I wrote a book when I was quite young, maybe ten years old. I didn't know anything about publishing. All I knew was that publishers published books. I did not know it was a highly selective process. I did not know that certain publishers published certain types of books. I just knew this—they rejected my work.

I was devastated.

I was ten years old and overly sensitive. Like a turtle, I pulled my head back into my shell, determined to never write a book again. But I kept filling up with words, stories, lessons—all of which I desired to share. All of which I believed would help others.

In writing this book, I had to fight with my ten year old self and let her know that she was healed and that God would indeed rule and protect me (and her) on this journey. I refer to the ten year old and the present me because we both live together within me.

My childhood lessons have a huge voice. They direct my actions as long as I allow them to. Childhood is where all our first and most influential decisions, decrees and declarations were made. They have become the foundation for all our lives. The culture I grew up in, the things I heard and saw, the reactions to what I said or did— all of this helped me shape my decisions, decrees, and declarations before I knew that is what I was doing.

But even in light of my childhood pain from rejection, I ached to get this story out. The concept of it overwhelmed my days. I researched information about diamonds. I got stuck on commercials about them. I sang songs about them and I kept seeing the tie in between me and a diamond. The words, the theme, and the significance of the gem would not leave me alone. I finally told the ten year old me, "You'll be okay. God promises to heal and protect you. He is with us!" I had to direct my self talk in a godly direction since I wanted godly results.

The pressure of needing to advance when the scared and scarred little girl in me wanted to retreat is what took me so long to get this out. I had to trust God in my fears and through to my victory.

Nevertheless, the battle between remaining silent and content with the way my life was going and releasing what I am purposed to do continued to rage. I was disquieted, disgruntled, and dismayed. My defiance ultimately yielded to my destiny and I began to write. The pressure I endured pushed me into the process of change.

Pressure pushes us into a process. Just as a diamond is violently propelled from seclusion into exposure, your process propels you into the best and brightest version of yourself if you allow it to do so. I encourage you to submit to the process.

***

Think about it

What images come to mind when you hear the word process?

_____

_____

_____

_____

_____

_____

_____

_____

_____

_____

_____

_____

_____

_____

_____

_____

_____

_____

_____

When you think of pressure, what thoughts or words come to mind?

_____

_____

_____

_____

_____

_____

_____

_____

_____

_____

_____

_____

_____

_____

Prayer

Father, I want to look at pressure in a new way. Help me to see it differently. Help me turn to you both for protection and direction. Though I'm afraid and want to fight against this process, I want your help. I want the godly response so I need Heaven's download. Help.

3

YOUR G.E.M. PERIOD

I will give you hidden treasures, riches stored in secret places so that you may know that I am the LORD, the God of Israel, who summons you by name. - Isaiah 45:3

GESTATION

Anyone who is a parent, especially mothers, understand this term. It is the time where a baby at its very start begins to absorb all that it needs. It's hidden in the safety of the womb.

Like a developing child, a diamond gets its start in the "womb" of the earth. This is where it grows and begins the process of being a beautiful precious stone.

Gestation is an unseen time for a baby and a diamond. It becomes accustomed to the environment. It is nourished, grows and is protected. It is completely unaware that it is getting ready to enter a completely different environment in a very violent and abrupt manner.

Like that diamond, you are being nourished and moving into something dynamically new and totally different from what you have experienced in the past. Diving into yourself and asking questions will help you adjust to this environment and give you tools and foundation on which you can both rest and stand.

***

Think about it

Are you currently in a gestation period? How do you know? What are the signs?

_____

_____

_____

_____

_____

_____

_____

_____

_____

_____

_____

_____

_____

_____

_____

_____

_____

_____

_____

_____

_____

What lessons have you learned from being in your gestation period?

_____

_____

_____

_____

_____

_____

_____

_____

_____

_____

_____

_____

_____

What do you now know about yourself and your gifts?

_____

_____

_____

_____

_____

_____

_____

_____

_____

_____

His Word/My Thoughts

_____

_____

_____

_____

_____

_____

_____

_____

_____

_____

_____

_____

_____

EXCAVATION

To excavate is to remove from a cavity—a low or hidden place. As a diamond, God has had to excavate you with force from the cocoon of your own making. From your own comfort. That excavation probably felt like your life exploded; like every relationship around you just erupted. It was violent and unexpected. It hurt. It traumatized you (momentarily). But when the excavation is over, you are exposed to a new world and a new experience. The time for you to sparkle and shine has just begun!

Take heart! Even if you did not expect to be removed from where you are, there is a Divine plan that comes with this excavation. Like a newborn, you may wonder what this new world is and may feel ill-equipped to handle your new environment. But the breath of life has been exhaled into you. You will adjust and soon thrive in this new life. Being in a different place is uncomfortable but, just like the newborn, it is necessary to live. Just like a diamond, it's necessary to shine. Being excavated is purposeful for the Master, so it is beneficial and necessary for you. Like the newborn baby being swaddled for warmth and protection know this, He is with you.

***

Think about it

Are you in a position of comfort from which you need to be removed or need to remove yourself? Describe what that position is — be detailed.

_____

_____

_____

_____

_____

_____

_____

_____

_____

_____

_____

_____

_____

_____

_____

_____

_____

_____

Can you recall an event that pushed you out from, or excavated you, from a place of comfort? Write about it.

_____

_____

_____

_____

_____

_____

_____

_____

_____

_____

_____

_____

_____

_____

_____

_____

_____

_____

_____

_____

_____

_____

_____

_____

_____

_____

His Word/My Thoughts

_____
_____
_____
_____
_____
_____
_____
_____
_____
_____
_____
_____

MOTIVATION

Everyone needs a good personal push (motivation). Motivation is the reason you do something. We go get food because we are motivated by our hunger. We pay our bills because we want to maintain the service we receive or the product we purchased. Those are some straightforward examples. Dreams, however, can be a little more challenging when trying to maintain our motivation.

When it comes to food and bills, there is an obvious motivation. With a dream, it is not always the same. In fact, if you and I don't take some time to deal with our "why," it can be very easy to put off going for our dreams.

The first step to maintaining a consistent motivation is knowing your purpose. Ask yourself, "What am I here to do? The second step is knowing no purpose is small. Don't measure your dream or gifts against others. The third step—and the most critical—is understanding your WHY. The motivation to do what you are called to do, to pursue your dreams, comes AFTER you know your purpose and accept your assignment. For me, I know I am here to help people. I came to realize how much joy came to me when I helped people. I can literally feel myself more grounded. Because of this, I am always asking myself, how can I serve the people? What can I bring them? On the other side, when I am not engaged, when I'm not helping, I feel pain; a pain that I don't have words to describe. It is an emptiness and a separation from living I never want to return to. That "why" keeps me motivated to continue to walk in my calling.

Here's the bottom line when it comes to motivation: You must embrace the fact that the pleasure of living your purpose and achieving your dream provides a satisfaction that you will have never known before. You also must understand that extreme pain comes with not doing operating in your purpose. Not working on your dream hurts. For a long time.

You see, God has placed his desires in our hearts. How can we comfortably sit and not move forward in those desires? Think about it! The perfect one said, "I need her/him/them!" He took the time to form us; to place gifts within us.

God set you in a particular place and time. He allowed or gave you experiences. He has a one of a kind way for you to do what you do. As I think about this, it motivates me into action. What God says about me is true. It moves me into action to think that God thinks that much of me. If *he* believes it, I do too. We must begin to give time in prayer and meditation to his thoughts and plans for each of us (see Jer. 29:11). Then we must put his strategy in place as he continues to breathe on his good plan for our lives.

Each and every diamond has a purpose, dream, and assignment. Every one of them—including you! Each one is different, unique, and necessary!

Why motivation? It is the fuel in the engine of your dream. It is our glimpse of the plan of God for our lives. Motivation is what keeps the diamond under the hand of the Master as it is shaped and brought into its ultimate sparkle and shine. Motivation is the constant whisper and the present fragrance that says, "Go on, Diamond! Shine!"

Motivation is the next level. It's sometimes pushy and annoying. Sometimes we push down or medicate our motivation because it is disturbing. It is like an itch that screams "scratch me" or a sore muscle that shouts "ice me." With our dreams, we sometimes don't know in which direction to go. Or if we do, the results don't appear as quickly as we imagined. Being motivated is often the nudge that keeps us going when our steps are unsure and our paths cloudy.

So, what's your motivation? What is your *itch*? What is that sore muscle? Having a push is what keeps you going when you can't see clearly; when you can only feel your way through. When your dream, the end goal, is the only vision you have, motivation is your walking stick.

Take some time to write out your dream and don't be overwhelmed OR underwhelmed by its size.

***

Think about it

What is your big dream?

_____

_____

_____

_____

_____

_____

_____

_____

_____

_____

_____

Why must this dream happen? Be detailed!

_____

_____

_____

_____

_____

_____

_____

_____

_____

_____

_____

_____

_____

_____

_____

_____

_____

_____

_____

_____

_____

_____

_____

_____

_____

His Word/My Thoughts

_____

_____

_____

_____

_____

_____

_____

_____

_____

_____

_____

_____

Prayer

Father, you numbered my days and knew me before I was even born. Help me move. Help me take hold of the exposure into new territory and equip me to do all you've called me to do. You created me for a reason. Let it be real and realized. I am yours to use. I dwell beneath your shadow and am covered by your wings. I am confident in You.

4

COLOR

I praise you because I am fearfully and wonderfully made.
Your works are wonderful, I know that full well.
Psalms 139:14

My history is one of being surrounded by helpers. They came in the form of teachers and coaches. To this day, many of my relatives hold positions that in one way or another teach and/or coach. In my home, growing up, my mother worked in personnel and my father (as mentioned before) volunteered as a football coach. Both my parents had integral parts of shaping the lives of others and helping them to discover hidden potential and gifts.

Additionally, I was always encouraged to speak as a child. My grandfather never told me "children should be seen and not heard." He said, "do your research, form an opinion, and then speak." We are all talkers in my family, largely due to this challenge from my grandfather.

Around the dinner table, we all engaged in the sharing of information, stories, and so much more. There was a great deal of politics, history ,and opinion at that table (and more food than I can describe). In many ways, encouraging this sharing was a way of empowering each of us. If we knew more, we could do more. It was certainly a different way of saying "I love you" but it was always meant and understood to be a strong sentiment, an endearing action. This is the "ground" I grew up in. These are the "nutrients" in the soil of my life. This is what has given me the "color" others see in me today.

The elders in my family wanted to send us out into the world with knowledge and the ability to be strategic in how it was used. I want to do the same for you. Think of it as my own "I love you."

The color of a diamond is based on the nutrients in its gestational ground. Many will end up becoming the colorless diamond (the most familiar), but others will be red, blue, green, or even yellow. No matter what, the color is based on the diamond's surroundings. The same goes for you.

The "ground" (community, culture, traditions) you were raised in has colored your life. Now is the time to choose how you will let this coloring affect you. Will you be confined by it or conquer it?

There is something to learn and gather from everything in our lives, even if it is learning what to throw away. As we submit to the process of being shaped and examined, we ultimately grow into who we are. Confidently confronting our history helps to celebrate the victory of our lives instead of continually mourning our tragedies. As challenging as this may seem, there is a healthy way to get through each challenge that colors you.

***

Think about it

Are you willing to come face to face with the challenging things that have colored your life? If so, describe what these challenges are and how each has affected you.

_____

_____

_____

_____

_____

_____

_____

_____

_____

_____

_____

_____

_____

_____

_____

_____

_____

_____

_____

_____

_____

_____

_____

How will you use the "colors" of your life (experiences, tragedies, challenges) to bless and encourage others?

_____

_____

_____

_____

_____

_____

_____

_____

_____

_____

_____

_____

_____

_____

_____

_____

_____

_____

_____

_____

_____

_____

_____

_____

His Word/My Thoughts

_____

_____

_____

_____

_____

_____

_____

_____

_____

_____

_____

_____

_____

_____

Prayer

Father, you've placed some things in my life. Some I understand and others, if I'm honest, I don't. But what I am sure of is your goodness and that you have a plan for my life. Those things that will not be taken away, let them be marked by you. Let me declare your goodness and healing over what I cannot change and what marks me as a submitted vessel. I trust your choices and know that whatever color I am, it stands for victory.

5
CUT

He cuts off every branch in me that bears no fruit, while every branch that does bear fruit he prunes so that it will be even more fruitful.
John 15:2

I've been cut many times. In each circumstance, the cut pushed me into purpose. A while ago, I served as a life coach for a long term rental assistance program. I had the distinct privilege of helping people (usually single moms) pull together their finances. Most importantly, I helped them explore why they got into the situation that led them to the assistance program in the first place. It was a deep personal dive for each of these people. All their stories moved and challenged me, sometimes bringing me to tears. Each person allowed me into some of the most personal parts of their lives. They trusted me with their stories and so did God. One day I was informed that the grant tht made my position possible, would no longer be available. I was being cut.

I was only slightly bothered initially, but by the last day of the program, I was inconsolable. My clients cried and, this time, I cried with them. My employer released me to go home.

This particular cut made me see how I'd placed the full weight of this help for others on myself. My job had become my sole source for fulfilling this part of my purpose. As I said, I am a helper. But I'd gotten a little too comfortable in my position so when it was taken away, I struggled with that. I had to repent and promise God that, the next time around, I would partner with *him* in all my helping. I am now beginning an outreach program for women called *Her Harvest*. And guess what? All the workshops and connections I'd built up during my time at the agency are now continuing and expanding this new program. So yes, I was a cut. But this cut allows me to move in purpose knowing that it's God and me. He knew what it would take for me to make this move so he removed what was hindering me. What remained exposed something new in beauty and form.

A master gemologist examines a diamond. They know how to get the greatest sparkle and shine from the raw gem. They understand its characteristics and know its flaws. They work to bring out the beauty of the diamond. Each diamond is different and requires an expert to bring out its beauty.

When a diamond is cut, part of what it is disappears. It's gone forever. As a person, this concept challenges us and gives us pause. Cutting off parts of your life…well…it hurts! But it is needed. You will be cut. Cut off from people, places and things. But you will be better, stronger, and perfected as a result.

As you consider the "Master" gemologist, know that He indeed knows what is best and necessary to bring about the best sparkle and shine in you.

***

Think about it

What must you release and allow to be cut out of your life in order to get the best sparkle and shine?

_____

_____

_____

_____

_____

_____

Is there something that has already been cut from your life that you can see is allowing the best and brightest to come out in you?

_____

_____

_____

_____

_____

_____

_____

_____

_____

_____

_____

_____

_____

_____

_____

_____

_____

_____

_____

_____

_____

_____

_____

His Word/My Thoughts

_____

_____

_____

_____

_____

_____

_____

_____

_____

_____

_____

_____

_____

Prayer

Father, you know exactly what needs to be cut out of my life. I don't like it sometimes. I'm even afraid, to be honest. I've held on to these things for so long, but I trust you. Cut those things out of my life and shape me as you have designed. You know what is best.

You love me and I submit to the cutting.

6

CLARITY

But he said to me, My grace is sufficient for you, for my power is made perfect in weakness,
Therefore I will boast all the more gladly about my weaknesses,
so that Christ's power may rest on me.
II Corinthians 12:9

I am a super sensitive soul. It has definitely been a journey handling this part of me. There was a time when I wanted to be different. I wanted to be unmoved by comments people made about me or others. My attempts to model the behavior of others who were better at managing their emotions did not work. I just ended up being even more ridiculous than before.

Because hurt feelings come easily, I have learned to do a few things to help myself in my own process.

(1) I limit my exposure to some people
(2) I talk myself through and out of being hurt
(3) I ask God how he wants these sensitivities to be used.

A diamond's clarity is actually based on its blemishes (sometimes called birthmarks or inclusions). The greater the blemish, the lower the clarity. The opposite is true for people.

You see, God created me sensitive and so my sensitivities have a purpose. During the cutting phase, some inclusions in my diamond life are eliminated but others remain. Being extra sensitive is an inclusion in my life that I've grown to understand has great purpose.

My vulnerability allows others to get real with their own personal pain. My sensitivity means I'm likely to call a person at just the right time. I will give them permission to cry because tears do not scare me. The acceptance of our blemishes/inclusions can turn into a testimony that give someone else the courage to accept their own weaknesses. We will find, just like the apostle Paul did in the scripture at the opening of this chapter, that God's grace is sufficient.

According to Hebrews 12:1, we can set aside the sin and weight that easily hinders us. We have the ability to let go of our blemishes. And unlike diamonds, by doing this, we can have the greatest level of clarity possible.

Could it be that your unwillingness to embrace the life package you've been given is causing you to lose some sparkle and shine? Life comes with its givens. Your choice to embrace your blemishes and accept them, allows you the opportunity for the greatest level of brilliance.

***

Think about it

Can you identify something you were born with that would be considered a personality blemish? Is it something you should allow to be cut OR might it serve a greater purpose by remaining a part of your life?

_____

_____

_____

_____

_____

_____

_____

_____

_____

_____

_____

_____

_____

_____

_____

_____

_____

_____

_____

_____

_____

_____

Are you willing to submit this thing to God and allow him to show you the beauty even in that? What is the after effect of your prayer of submission?

_____

_____

_____

_____

_____

_____

_____

_____

_____

_____

_____

_____

_____

_____

_____

_____

_____

_____

_____

_____

_____

_____

_____

_____

_____

_____

His Word/My Thoughts

_____

_____

_____

_____

_____

_____

_____

_____

_____

_____

_____

_____

_____

_____

Prayer

Father, I never realized that my frailties and were truly part of your design for me. There have been some things I didn't like about me. I've wanted more of this or less of that. I understand now that you made me after your design, in both fear and wonder. I never thought you needed me to look and be only me. Forgive me for not considering that those things I didn't care for were actually a unique design, tailor made for me. Help me to hold on to this truth and let go of hurtful self-hating thoughts.

7

CARAT

But the pot he was shaping from the clay was marred in his hands; so the potter formed it into another pot shaping it as seemed best to him.
Jeremiah 18:4

My experiences have shaped me. I think one of the most painful experiences was the loss of my parents. There is a pulling in me. One part of me existed in the depths of sorrow. I mentioned earlier how close my parents and I were. The other side was relieved that they were no longer in physical pain and the ravages of their illnesses could no longer attack them. No one wants those they love to suffer. Yet, at the end of both of these feelings, I was alone. For the first time, I felt more alone than I had ever experienced before. This loneliness shaped me.

I made many mistakes in my pain. Poor decisions that followed me for years by way of consequence. I alienated some that should have remained close and held others close that should have been left alone. I cried, got sick, put on mask after mask, and finally cried out to God. He heard me and carried me through a personal and intimate process. God heard me. He healed me and he let me know I held value. No matter what, I was still priceless.

The weight of a diamond is referred to as a carat. The carat weight has less to do with the size than it does with other characteristics such as its crown and its cut (pear, oval, heart, etc.)

All of the processes that you and I go through helps to determine our weight. In Christ, none of us are lightweights. The sum total of our journey adds to who and what we are and how that purpose gets played out in our lives. Our carat weight, if you will, helps others know our story. As you share what you have experienced with a neighbor or an audience, the value of your life comes through and it helps others have the strength to continue. Your carat weight, in the form of your testimony, is an enduring echo of how God has enabled you to shine.

***

Think About it

Your assignment carries weight. Are you clear on your life assignment (what God has called you to do)? Take some time to write it out.

_____

_____

_____

_____

_____

_____

_____

_____

_____

_____

_____

_____

Who will benefit from you completing your assignment?

_____

_____

_____

_____

_____

_____

_____

_____

_____

_____

_____

_____

His Word/My Thoughts

_____

_____

_____

_____

_____

_____

_____

_____

_____

_____

Prayer

Father, you made me for a reason. As I journey through life, my desire is to know the reason, embrace it and fulfill the call. Help me to stay focused on what you have given me to do and not compare myself to others. My assignment is tailor made for me. I rejoice in knowing you took the time to make it for me. No matter the size of the assignment, I realize that every one of them has significant impact on the Kingdom.

I rejoice in knowing I am a part of the impact.

8

FACET

In the same way, let your light shine before others that they may see your good deeds and
glorify your Father in heaven.
Matthew 5:16

Some of the darkest days of my life came from carrying burdens that were not mine to carry. Trying to fix people is a God sized job that I tried to take on. BIG MISTAKE! I can remember at six years old trying to solve a problem; a huge issue between my grandfather and one of my uncles. Two things are true: my grandfather should not have shared this with a small child and I was way too immature to help. But I was also too immature to realize my shortcomings. It took me many years, even decades, before I gave up and turned over my family, friends, and everything else to God.

The loss of my parents? Gave it to God. The clinging to people whose time in my life had expired? Gave it and them to God. I realized there really was nothing I needed to handle on my own and that the weight belonged to God and God alone. When I decided to let go, the pain started to lift. When the pain lifted, the darkness subsided and that's when it happened: I sparkled and shined.

I had to allow more time with God and to be specific, I had to really talk with him about how I felt. Unfortunately, I was really good at studying, teaching, going to service, and doing ministry all without really being open with God. Isn't it funny how we can go through the motions in the faith? We can look the part without capturing and enjoying all the benefits. In those moments, most of the things we do in a church become just something to do. We might have moments of clarity and honesty with God and that is great, but it doesn't last because we haven't been real with him. Truly yearning and seeking that time with him daily is what God desires from us. Everything else should grow out of that personal interaction.

In that still space of daily devotion, there is wisdom and instruction available. There is light and an unveiling of truth. There is even a way to solutions and healing. As we look into the light of His word and spend time in his presence, we freely release our darkness. This leaves space for his light to come to us and pour out from us. All of this is wrapped up in the process of being a diamond. It's simple and complex all at the same time.

A facet is a diamond's interaction with light based on its cut. The diamond is masterfully cut because of the precision. When it comes into contact with light, it sparkles and shines. Each facet attracts others to it. What has happened to you, the things you allowed to be cut, your color, all of it, will attract others to you and will allow you to share your story.

Will you consider the brightness of your future and the way you will shine in the light? When the issues that scar you, the stuff that doesn't serve you, has been cut away, and you have endured the process, the light will shine so brightly from you that it will reveal and reflect the intimacy of your relationship with God.

***

Think about it

How have you seen letting go of past limiting behaviors improve your connection with God (hearing/development/wisdom)? What was the result?

_____

_____

_____

_____

_____

_____

_____

_____

_____

_____

_____

_____

_____

_____

_____

_____

_____

_____

_____

_____

_____

_____

His Word/My Thoughts

_____

_____

_____

_____

_____

_____

_____

_____

_____

_____

_____

_____

_____

Prayer

Father, you have made it safe for me to let go and you have shown me the results of allowing you to come into my dark places. Walk me out of them and reveal your light to me. I desire wisdom. I want to hear you and obey. I want to act on your command. Help me as I come to you. You are my source.

9

REFLECTION

You yourselves are our letter, written on our hearts,
known and read by everyone.
II Corinthians 3:2

I am often met with the comment, "There is just something special about you." Sometimes I hear this at the store, other times at an event or social function. Initially this made me a little nervous. Then vanity made me think about my hair style, makeup or outfit, as if this combination of exterior things was the only possible meaning of the statement. Eventually, I came to myself. I now know better.

To borrow a Mary Mary lyric, "It's the God in me."

There is a presence of God that comes upon a believer as he/she/they walk out their belief. The more I walk out my faith, the more I trust God and walk out my purpose. The more I walk out my purpose, the more I sparkle and shine. I am God's reflection on the earth.

Reflection means *to bend back*. Its root word is *flexible*. A diamond reflects on or bends back its image in the face of light. We do the exact same thing. The purpose of our sparkle and shine is to reflect God.

When you read *sparkle and shine*, I'm talking about the unveiling of the individual beauty you were meant to be. This is beauty beyond eyes, skin, hair, and lips. This is soul beauty.

No, it's not about being seen. It's about realizing, embracing and celebrating YOU. There's only one you. The mold has been broken, the assignment given, and the way opened.

Each one of us must allow the cut, color, clarity and carat of our lives to bend back or point back to the light of Jesus.

***

Think about it

Think of a time where you realized you were reflecting God. What was the experience? What do you think about it now?

_____

_____

_____

_____

_____

_____

_____

_____

_____

_____

_____

_____

_____

_____

What has been the result of reflecting God's image? Think of a specific example.

_____

_____

_____

_____

_____

_____

_____

_____

_____

_____

_____

_____

_____

_____

What are two to three things you can do daily to reflect God's image?

_____

_____

_____

_____

_____

_____

_____

_____

_____

_____

What does it mean to you to sparkle and shine?

_____

_____

_____

_____

_____

_____

_____

_____

_____

_____

How does it make you feel to know that God made only one of you and he is pleased?

_____

_____

_____

_____

_____

_____

_____

_____

_____

_____

What will you do to solidify and embrace your uniqueness?

_____
_____
_____
_____
_____
_____
_____
_____
_____
_____

How did you feel being removed from a place of comfort? What good came from it or what do you hope to gain from being removed from a place of comfort?

_____
_____
_____
_____
_____
_____
_____
_____
_____
_____

His Word/Your Thoughts

_____

_____

_____

_____

_____

_____

_____

_____

_____

_____

_____

_____

_____

Prayer

Father, help me to see and embrace me. I am the one and only me and I delight in learning more and more each day. I thank you for making me in fear and wonder and for giving me my own assignment. Give me opportunities to use that assignment to point those I meet to you. God, I pray in the name of Jesus, that each day I would be flexible and bend back under your hand. That Your light radiating from me would point back to you and encourage others to sparkle and shine as you have enabled me to sparkle and shine!

10

Settings

And God raised us up with Christ and seated us with him
in heavenly realms in Christ Jesus.
Ephesians 2:6

Having the right perspective gives us a critical advantage in life. In my most successful negotiations, in both personal and professional settings, perspective has helped me to succeed. I define success as any circumstance or scenario where everyone in the relationship or interaction wins. To accomplish this, we often after to change our perspective. I can't think of any better perspective than heaven's. The scripture above lets us know we can attain a heavenly perspective in life. How we see things has a direct effect on how we feel about things. And how we feel about things informs how we respond to them.

As I continue to go through this process, I recognize one thing. My responses to life nowadays are very different from might have said and did in times past. Becoming a diamond is about maturing and sometimes, maturing hurts. With every turn, as I allow myself to be cut, I understand the most essential thing: life is work. We wake up to work each day—the work of living the abundant life in Christ.

Christ allows us to sit with him. He wants to be our foundation and for us to see what he sees, the way he sees it. This goes beyond being sensitive and into being obedient and action oriented. All of us are obedient to something and we act out of that obedience. The real question is, what or who are you obedient to and how does that obedience determine your actions?

I got a life changing call on June 30, 2016. I had taken a vacation day so the human resources specialist at my former employer called me at home. The grant that supported my job was not renewed. I was unemployed...again. Working at a job that is grant supported is always an exercise in faith. You can do your best and someone else's decision stops you in your tracks. In that moment, I had to decide who was in charge. I had to have a heavenly mindset and figure out what Heaven was saying. I had to decide that this new event to me, was no surprise God. He was not in Heaven scratching his head saying "What are we gonna do now?" He was not disturbed or distraught. He had moved on to the next part of the plan for me. So I had to decide where I wanted to sit. Was I going to sit with him? Was I going to trust that God indeed knew what he was doing? And watch this: if I sat with him in heavenly places, I would inevitably find out what the next "play" would be.

I chose to take my seat there with Christ.

I won't say that it was just that simple or smooth. I won't say I didn't have questions about what happened. I will say I chose to take the right seat. I began to think about the good work that had been done. I thought about how I'd met young people who I never would have met without this program. A number of them, I still see and talk to today. I thought about the lessons they taught me and what I was able to share with them. Most of all, I thought "God loves all of them more than any of us love them." Again, he was not surprised and the same way he was moving me to the next thing, he would move them too.

In my past, I'm sure I would desperately tried to figure this out. I am a planner and am very solution oriented. This time though, I let the past be the past and prepared myself to move on to the next thing. Letting the past be the past is a growth area for me. I love history. But I have learned that doing a deep dive into my own is not always the best idea. How much history do I need? I have learned it is great to look at your history if you are either searching for a pattern of behavior and are willing to change the behavior. Anything beyond that and dwelling on the past gets dangerous.

It's a perspective that we cannot afford to have as diamonds.

When we rest on the past, we can romanticize what happened. We can make it better than it was or worse. Personally, I find neither are good or helpful. I find sitting where Christ sits to be the very best foundation for movement. We all see things better from a higher vantage point; from a mature perspective.

As I mature, I am able to laugh at myself more. I can be brutally honest and real with myself and even tell myself to stop talking! That wasn't always the case. I am sure I have helped to maintain some balance by doing this, even if just for myself. This diamond has chosen a heavenly setting.

Every diamond rests in some type of setting. There are all kinds of styles, but each rests in a setting. I like to think of it as a foundation. A foundation holds up a structure. Let your foundation be Christ. Let him hold you up. Let him be the place where you rest.

***

Think about it

What does it mean for you to be seated with Christ in heavenly places?

_____

_____

_____

_____

_____

_____

_____

_____

_____

_____

_____

When faced with a challenge, how might looking at it from a heavenly perspective direct a response better?

_____

_____

_____

_____

_____

_____

_____

_____

_____

_____

_____

His Word/Your Thoughts

_____

_____

_____

_____

_____

_____

_____

_____

_____

_____

AFTERWORD

YOU ARE UNDAUNTED, UNCONQUERABLE, & UNBREAKABLE

I have been a Christian for decades and initially, the thought of not going to hell sustained me. I was happy to read the bible, go to church and learn "Christianese" (the rote language of those who've been in the faith for a long time). One question gnawed at me though: Am I living the abundant life?

I knew the answer was no.

I didn't feel like "more than a conqueror" as Romans 8:37 said I should. I felt like less than one. I felt defeated. And it wasn't just a feeling. I *was* defeated. Because that's the way I thought, that's what my life reflected back to me.

Of course I knew that every day couldn't bring with it the promise of happiness and no struggles. It wasn't that I thought I shouldn't have problems. It was just that I didn't seem to handle them well. I knew everyone had *issues*, but I didn't handle mine well. I knew I would face challenges, it just never seemed to come to a good end. I was only existing. And even that existence seemed to be one lived on life support.

In hindsight, one of the most frightening things to consider is that no one really ever said anything to me. It seemed like no one noticed. Some may have been held from speaking by the Holy Spirit, but others never seemed to notice I had a problem. They seemed to admire my ability to get things done. Even worse, some counted on my need for approval. But I blame none of them. I am accountable for my life. I had to step up, put the big girl panties on, and put in the work of change.

I didn't want to remain sad and lowly. I wanted more and I knew God wanted more for me. I had to change the way I thought. I had to change my vision.

In Psalm 73, David laments about the prosperity of the wicked. He doesn't get why they prevail at all. I didn't understand it either. But I took another tip from David. In this same psalm, he says he saw their undoing when he went into the sanctuary. When I went into "the sanctuary" of my own soul, I saw things differently too.

I think we fear having intimacy with God. No matter how many of us have read that our "father in heaven gives good gifts to those who ask him" (Matt 7:11), they are too often just words we parrot instead of truths we live. I had to change, so the way I spent time with God had to change.

I needed internal and personal strategies. I needed *plays*. These strategies would lead to victory on the inside. I began to understand that my transformation required God and I to sit together and write out my plays, much like I've asked you to do in this book. This, in part, is what prayer is all about. This is what building a relationship with God is about. He is not out *there* somewhere. He is near, close and within. I needed that. I needed to experience God; the good and loving father. I needed to hear him through his word and through our time together. It is amazing to think that the One who created everyone would take the time to talk with me; to s,urround me with his presence and be so happy to do so. My life is forever enriched. And I now have the evidence that I can do this again!

These sessions changed my prayer life. When we think of prayer, many things come to mind. We pray for healing for ourselves, loved ones, and maybe colleagues. We pray about situations we are going through. We pray for things we want. There is nothing wrong with any of this. It's just that God wants to give us more.

When we were born, we learned the culture of our family, neighborhood, and community. It was easy, right? All we had to do was watch. For the most part, we believed what we saw and heard. When we became born again, we needed to learn a new culture. This time it took much more effort. This time we had to undo laws and systems that we have lived with all our lives. We have a new meaning of love and a new understanding of forgiveness. When that is different from what you were raised with, the conflict is all too real. Jesus points to this when he says, "And you cancel the word of God in order to hand down your own tradition" (Matt. 7:13 NLT).

Ouch!

For me, I had to decide that I could respect and love my parents and community without disregarding godly precepts. How did I do it? I chose to spend time with the Father. We have to choose to hear him. We have to choose to ask questions about ourselves.

I began to ask those questions. I wanted to know what God had to say about me. I believed that I was more than a "wretch undone" in Christ. In fact, I was the righteousness of God in Christ Jesus (2 Corinthians 5:21). I began to use what I call "God words" about me. Here is one of my favorite verses when I think of God words:

"And behold, a voice from Heaven said, This is my beloved son, with whom I am well pleased." Matt. 3:17 ESV

At this point, Jesus had only been baptized. That's it. He hadn't done any miracles—nothing. The power here is this: God is already pleased with us. We don't have to prove we are worthy of love or approval. We just need to accept *his* love and approval.

Jesus goes into a spirit0led forty-day fast following this. There, he is tempted by the devil. At every turn, the devil questions his position saying, "If you are the son of God ..." Jesus was unbothered. He believed and accepted his position and offers us a model for how we should live. He knew what the Father had already said about him and so he did not flinch when who he was came into question. We must believe what God said about us and cancel all other descriptors.

How do we do it?

Well, you've gotten a great start by making it to the end of this book. Now you must believe what God said. Put into a mental prison any thought or high thing that exalts itself against the knowledge of God (see 2 Corinthians 10:5a) in your life. Personally, I would stop in the middle of any place and say out loud, "I imprison this thought because it doesn't line up with God's word. I have the right to keep you in prison until you are obedient to Christ" (2 Corinthians 10:5b). You might think that's strange but in that moment, I felt power — real power. And to think that all that time, I had accepted self-defeating thoughts. Thoughts that limited my ability to pursue my purpose full throttle. I believed things of me that God did not. No more! As I figuratively sat on God's lap, I learned to tap into his unfathomable love for me. A love that knows the mistakes I will make in five years, and loves me just the same.

Also, continue to pour through the scriptures. Both the Old and New Testaments. What used to look like God's wrath to me in certain passages, later revealed itself to be his great patience for his children. Every good parent gives rules and warnings. They even allow for some consequences to show up in the lives of those they love the most. Ultimately God always came through for his own. Search the word for passages that confirm this for you.

God says beautiful things about us. He is excited about our uniqueness. He promises protection and care and concern through the best and the worst of times. Cherish this knowledge. Turn off the volume on the opinions of others and the need to obtain approval. This is part of the journey to recognizing yourself as a diamond.

Here are two more precious verses I hope you will hold close to you as I do:

The LORD God is with you, the mighty warrior who saves. He will take great delight in you. In his love, he will no longer rebuke you, but will rejoice over you with singing. - Zephaniah 3:17

May you have power, together with all the Lord's holy people, to grasp how wide and long and high and deep is the love of Christ. - Ephesians 3:18
I can't say this enough. This takes work. You've begun some of that work already in this book. But you must continue on. It is so easy to hide behind the Cross. It's so easy to shout and dance and sing. But the true responsibility of being a Christian is sometimes hidden. Just as a raw diamond is hidden in the earth and goes through

great scrutiny and labor to become its very best, we must be willing to allow our partner and Father God show us who we are and then believe it and happily live it! The last thing I want to share with you is one more trait you share with a diamond: it's strength.

As a diamond, you are undaunted, unconquerable, and unbreakable.

You are undaunted because you recognize that life is always going to fluctuate (ups, downs, and sideways happenings). Matthew 6:22 says that "the eye is the lamp of the body; if your eye is healthy your whole body will be full of light." That light comes in the form of wisdom, clarity and identity.

Knowing who you are, your irrevocable value in God's Kingdom, your unchangeable office as His child (there is nothing higher), will all serve in keeping you focused. It doesn't stop the hits, the curves or the setbacks. It does give you the focus and mindset to get up quickly. Knowing that life is going to happen, keeps you from being surprised by it in the first place. This self-awareness will give you a shield that, sometimes, will eliminate some of the hits altogether. At the very least, it will give you the wisdom and strategy to handle the challenges when they come. Being undaunted pushes you to focus on where you are going.

You are unconquerable. The word of God says, "Thanks be to God who always causes us to triumph in Christ, and makes manifest the savor of his knowledge by us in every place" (2 Corinthians 2:14). And since the word declares it, you should too! If God always causes us to triumph, then with his tools, we will win in Christ. To win in Christ is to have a victory that lines up with a godly point of view. It means as you review what happens to you, you can clearly see how the victory you attain is clearly and magnificently directed by the hand of God. Winning in Christ leaves you and others with dignity. When we win in Christ, it is not at the expense of others. We will show up in him. We will fight in him. We will win in him. It certainly can look different than what is in our imaginations, but if God says he will give us the victory, he will. We are unconquerable in him and as we pursue him, hear the Holy Spirit, and become knowledgeable of his moves, we fight with skill and our wins are consistent and evident.

Diamonds were first used as weapons. A weapon can be offensive or defensive. The beauty of a diamond's defensive side is that you can strike it with great power and never damage it. As you and I continue to write and execute our plays, we will become resilient. We will stand in the midst of what otherwise might destroy us.

Note: this is not to suggest you stay to an abusive relationship.

This *is* saying you are more powerful than you may have ever imagined. Remember, in your weakness, he is made strong (2 Corinthians 12:9-11). Just think about this impossibly hard crystal that can cut glass without damaging itself! On offense, a diamond gets to the heart of the matter. It cuts with precision and it cuts clean. A diamond-tipped tool cuts through some of the most durable substances in the world and so can you!

Finally, we are unbreakable! With all of the beauty, romance, and glamour attached to a diamond, there is one more characteristic we must discuss: the diamond is unbreakable. 1 Corinthians 15:58 says "Let nothing move you. Always give yourselves fully to the work of the Lord because you know that your labor in the Lord is not in vain." In other words, keep fighting!

Being a diamond (accepting, knowing, living your "diamond-hood"), means you can't be broken. The process you went through was individually shaping you to be all that you were designed to be. It brought out your best qualities. You were made with purpose and shaped by the Master gemologist, God himself!

You will be tried. You will be challenged. You will face some things you never imagined. But you will hold it together. You will remain strong, sparkling, and substantial. You are unbreakable. You are a diamond.